FILTHY LABORS

FILTHY LABORS

POEMS

LAUREN MARIE SCHMIDT

CURBSTONE BOOKS
NORTHWESTERN UNIVERSITY PRESS
EVANSTON, ILLINOIS

Curbstone Books
Northwestern University Press
www.nupress.northwestern.edu

Printed in the United States of America

10 9 8 7 6 5 4 3 2 1

Library of Congress Cataloging-in-Publication Data

Names: Schmidt, Lauren (Poet), author.
Title: Filthy labors : poems / Lauren Marie Schmidt.
Description: Evanston, Illinois : Curbstone/Northwestern University Press, 2017.
Identifiers: LCCN 2016045658| ISBN 9780810134690 (pbk. : alk. paper) |
ISBN 9780810134706 (e-book)
Subjects: LCSH: Homeless mothers—Poetry. | Women caregivers—Poetry. | Families—Poetry.
Classification: LCC PS3619.C44575 F55 2017 | DDC 811.6—dc23
LC record available at https://lccn.loc.gov/2016045658

For those ten mothers and their children—
wherever this may find you

CONTENTS

ACKNOWLEDGMENTS

Aethlon: Journal of Sports Literature "Memorial Park"

Big River Poetry Review "My Parents' New House, One Year after Hurricane Sandy"

The Citron Review "Parany"

Compose: A Journal of Simply Good Writing "Paterson"

Cutthroat "The Truth About Dionna"

Fifth Wednesday Journal "The Fourth of July," "Receiving"

Foliate Oak Literary Magazine "Brittany's Tattoo," "Inheritance," "On Route 208"

HEArt: Human Equity through Art "How We Go"

Lips "Some Joy"

Mobius: The Journal of Social Change "The English Teacher Gets a Lesson in Inference"

The Monmouth Review "The Nursing Home"

The New Verse News "Bastard Ghazal for the Death of SNAP"

North American Review "Faith," "Initiations," "Looking for Whitman," "The Room Toss Villanelle"

The Old and New Project "Unto Others," "Welfare Mothers"

Painted Bride Quarterly "The Box Marked 'F'"

Paterson Literary Review "Before Grief," "Expectations," "Grandpa's 70th Birthday," "Paterson," "The Social Worker's Advice"

The Progressive "In Defense of Poetry," "The Mother Called Meh-lay-gross"

Rattle "My Father Asks Me to Kill Him"

Southern Anti-Racism Network "Ladies' Day at the Playhouse"

Wormwood "Second Drink," "Till Death"

"Cloistered," "Faith," "Mother Teresa, Our Dearly Beloved Mother," "Receiving," and "Unto Others" were published as part of an essay written for the anthology *The Necessary Poetics of Atheism: Essays and Poems* (Sherman: Ill.: Twelve Winters Press, 2016).

Filthy Labors was a finalist for the 2016 Brittingham and Pollak Prizes from the University of Wisconsin Press.

"The Fourth of July," "Silver Alert," "Some Joy," and "What I Learned about My Father One Day at the Beach in 1986" are featured in an anthology of New Jersey poets, *Palisades, Parkways, and Pinelands* (Cliffwood, N.J.: Blast Press, 2016).

"Initiations" was nominated for a 2016 Pushcart Prize.

"Looking for Whitman" was published in the anthology *The Great Sympathetic: Walt Whitman and the "North American Review"* (Cedar Falls, Iowa: North American Review Press, 2015).

"My Parents' New House, One Year after Hurricane Sandy" was published in the anthology *Howl of Sorrow: A Collection of Poetry Inspired by Hurricane Sandy* (Long Branch, N.J.: Long Branch Arts Council, 2015).

"The Room Toss Villanelle" was a finalist for the 2016 James Hearst Poetry Prize.

"Unto Others" and "Welfare Mothers" were published as part of an essay written for "The Poetry of Resistance: Imagining the Overthrow of Capitalist Oppression," a Left Forum conference at John Jay College of Criminal Justice, New York, May 2015.

Grateful acknowledgments are given to the following individuals:

Though they may never know this book exists, the young mothers I worked with at the Haven House deserve special mention: their courage and grace inspired many of the poems in this collection.

Thank you to the poets who visited the Haven House with me to share their work with the mothers there: Martín Espada, John Murillo, Luivette Resto, and Rich Villar. I can only hope the days you spent with the women were as memorable for you as they were for the women. Thank you for honoring your call to service, for doing what too few poets do!

Thank you to the River Read Reading Series in Red Bank, New Jersey, my first poetry home. A special shout-out to Linda Mulhausen and Gregg Glory for their endless support of my work.

Thanks to the founding poets of RAW at PCCC: Andre Brown, Miguel DeJesus, Hafeezah Goldsmith, Beki Hafelfinger, and Ronnie Moultrie. Keep writing, my fearless poets!

Thank you to my friends for being along for the ride: Chris Brandt, Alan Carl, Maria Mazziotti Gillan, Matt Hall, Josh Keiner, Mary Ann B. Miller, Jacqui Morton, Jeremy Schraffenberger, Mariana Sierra, Abigail Templeton-Greene.

Thank you to two very special mentors, Doug Anderson and Jim Daniels, who took the time to read these poems and this collection in various stages.

Thank you to Jennifer McMillan and Alan Ring, the only two nonpoets on this list and the two who've known me longer than anyone—in some ways, your support means the most.

And finally, I owe a huge debt of gratitude to Sam Hamill and Gianna Francesca Mosser, without whom this book would not have been possible. Are there any words for what you've done for me?

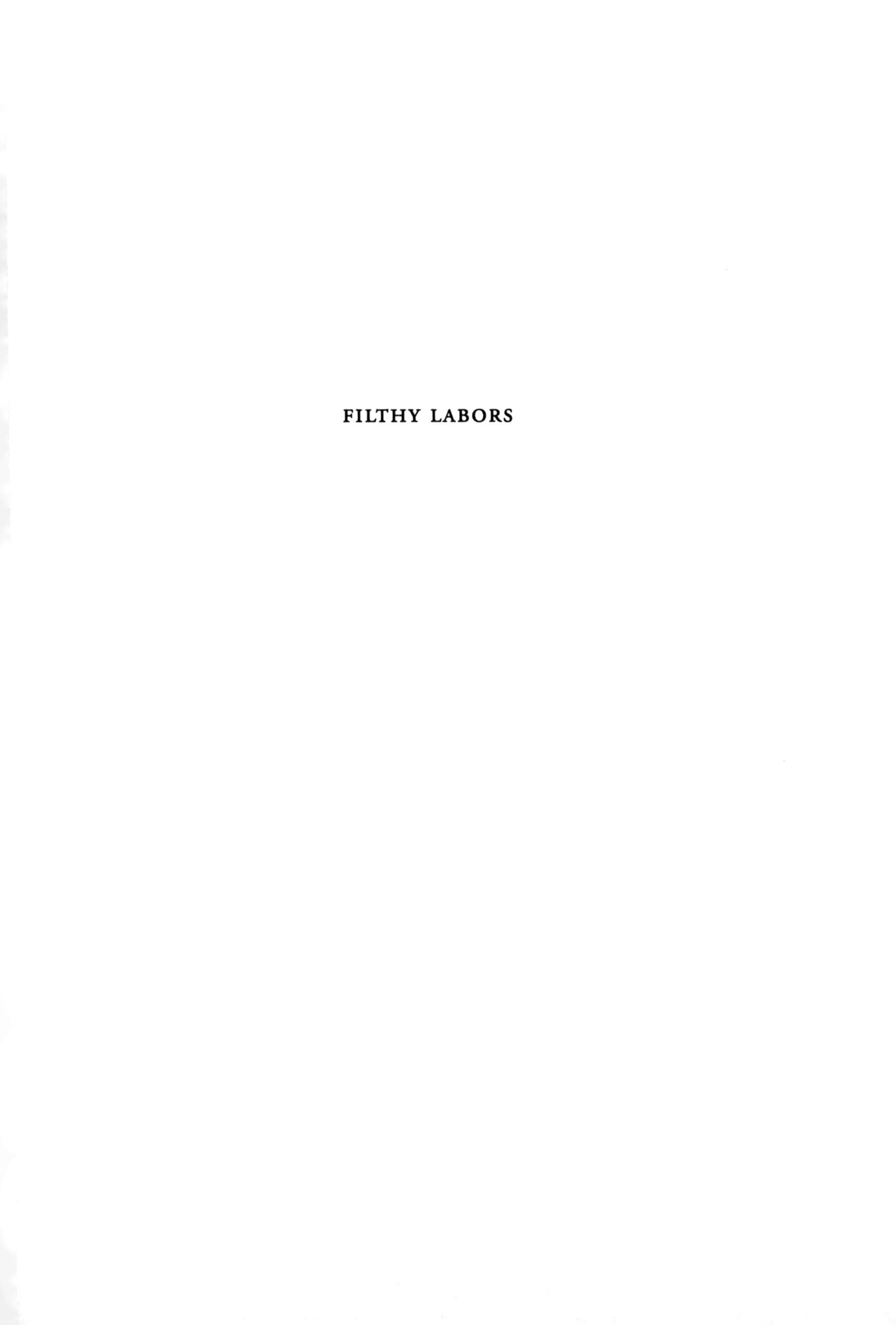

FILTHY LABORS

PART I
HOLY ORDERS

This is what you shall do: Love the earth and sun and the animals, despise riches, give alms to every one that asks, stand up for the stupid and crazy, devote your income and labor to others, hate tyrants, argue not concerning God, have patience and indulgence toward the people, take off your hat to nothing known or unknown or to any man or number of men, go freely with powerful uneducated persons and with the young and with the mothers of families.

—Walt Whitman, from the preface to *Leaves of Grass*

In Defense of Poetry

The Haven House for Homeless Women and Children

To you who say

poetry is a waste of ten homeless mothers' time—
that I should correct their grammar and spelling,
spit-shine their speech so it gleams, make them sound
more like me, that I should set a bucket of *Yes, miss,*
Thank you, Whatever you say, miss on their heads,
fill that bucket heavy, tell them how to tiptoe
to keep it steady, that I should give them something
they can truly use, like diapers, food, or boots—

I say

you've never seen these women lower their noses
over poetry, as if praying the rosary, as if hoping
for a lover to slip his tongue between their lips,
or sip a thin spring of water from a fountain.

PART II
PENANCE

As soon as histories are properly told there is no more need of romances.

—Walt Whitman, from the preface to *Leaves of Grass*

Paterson

Not just the spray lifting from the brink of the Great Falls, but
the busted, blood-red of brake lights in vacant lots,
the pennies circling the bottom of a hungry man's cup,
fire escapes, hose-watered sidewalks, the bars of storefront gates
rising at nine, the barbed wire spirals of the cellblocks
on Grand, iron bars guarding apartment windows,
slanted streetlamps, the rails that run into the heart of
and far from this city, the rooftops of vestigial silk mills—
these things, too, shine under sunlight.

How We Go

The Haven House for Homeless Women and Children

My babyfather passed away last night,
Jaslin whispered. *Passed away.* That phrase was my mother's the day
she sat at my bed's edge to wake me. She rested her hands
on my belly, sighed, *Grandpa passed away this morning,*
then trembled. *This is how we go*, I, at sixteen, believed: gently,
with family at your bedside. I tried to imagine what *passed away* looked like—
more peaceful than the look of the hair on my mother's unslept head,
her snot-nose and pinch-face—but, new to human death then,
I could only think of my silver fish, how its scaly skin skimmed the water,
how its tail fin drooped like a tired eyelid, how my dead pet limped over the lip
of the bowl I tilted above toilet water, the plink-splash
the corpse made, how water's resistance
slowed the fish's sinking.

You ain't gonna tell your child that, Q'nisha said, half asking.
She meant that Jaslin can't tell her daughter how her daddy died—
how a body bursts into bloody fish lips in thirteen places,
how car windows trap splattered bits of flesh, how slowly
gunshot skin slides down windshield glass. She can't tell her daughter
how Daddy's cotton shirt stuck to the gum of blood, how the radio
played and played before the cops came, how a boy
with a backpack saw everything and ran away.

No, tonight Jaslin will lower herself
to the edge of her daughter's bed and invent a story,
one where her father *passed away*. Tonight, a mother's words will fall
slowly, as if through water, and a child will burst the way
a balloon bursts at the kiss of a pin tip. Tonight,
a coroner will dab a dead father's wounds with gauze.

The Mother Called Meh-lay-gross

The Haven House for Homeless Women and Children

I know why the caged bird beats his wing
    Till its blood is red on the cruel bars;
For he must fly back to his perch and cling
When he fain would be on the bough a-swing;
    And a pain still throbs in the old, old scars
And they pulse again with a keener sting—
I know why he beats his wing!
—Paul Laurence Dunbar, "Sympathy"

It was a month before I met the mother the caseworkers
called Meh-lay-gross: *She can't write English enough to write
poetry,* I was told. *She won't want to participate anyway.
She doesn't like to be in the group for whatever reason.*
Not flesh, not hair, not voice, not eyes nor lips, not blood,
not bone, the mother the caseworkers called Meh-lay-gross
was just a name and *She can't, She won't, She doesn't.*

I imagine the mother the caseworkers called Meh-lay-gross
sitting upstairs in her room. All the other women and I talk
poetry at the common table, but while they lower their eyes
over notebooks, I scowl at the ceiling-high mural on the wall.
The image: three hands—one brown, one white, one black—
flung upwards, having released a dove to flight. To the right,
a manila scroll, half-unrolled, covered with the cursive words

of Angelou:
*The Caged Bird sings with a fearfull thrill
Of things unknown but longed for still
and his tune is heard on a distant hill
for the caged bird sings of freedom.*

Fearful misspelled with double *ll*'s and *thrill*, which should be *trill*:
no one corrected the errors because the lines are not about
clipped wings, nor *tied feet*, nor *bars of rage*; they are about
those three hands, that flying, that freedom. No other words
matter but freedom. So we study the rest of "I Know Why
the Caged Bird Sings," and all of Dunbar's "Sympathy,"
the *old, old scars* and the *keener sting*, then the mothers
write about their cages and why they think the caged

bird sings:
I cut myself cuz I am ugly and fat . . .
I wish I killed my baby then . . .
I think I might be pregnant again . . .
And upstairs sits Meh-lay-gross: *She can't, She won't, She doesn't.*

On the wall opposite the mural, a collage of quotes from great
white men—Shakespeare, Emerson, Thoreau—their timeless lines
about the persistent power of words. Wisdom written on the walls
of this place: the Haven House. This house, this manna, this sudden
and unexpected present, this windfall of aid and assistance, this blessing,
this boon from heaven, this gift from God on high. Inside, ten single women,
their infant children, fathers gone to other women, one dead, one in prison.
And upstairs sits Meh-lay-gross: *She can't, She won't, She doesn't.*

The first time I met the mother the caseworkers called Meh-lay-gross,
she stared at the white-lined paper and traced the margin's
long red line with the nail of her finger. She waited for words.
Eventually, she wrote a letter to me: *They no want me to speak Spanish*
to my daughter. I suppose to speak only in English. And is no OK with me.
In her office, a caseworker docks merit points for the mother's poor behavior.
And upstairs sits Milagros, breathing Spanish in her daughter's ear.

The English Teacher Gets a Lesson in Inference

The Haven House for Homeless Women and Children

You got any kids? Dionna asks.
No, I say, *I don't have any kids.*

You ever been pregnant?
I don't have any kids, so . . .

That ain't the question
that I asked you, she says.

Then she folds her arms across her chest
and waits for me to answer.

The Truth about Dionna

The Haven House for Homeless Women and Children

On my first day, when Anna the social worker said,
    I have a feeling you can handle yourself, she meant
I could handle myself against Dionna, specifically,
who had been kicked out of the house two times
before for swearing at the staff, who, Anna said,

will resist everything I try to do and so *Don't take it*
    personally. Don't let her scare you away.
It is true that on my first day, Dionna did nothing but glare
at me: she wouldn't read the poems, wouldn't write
her name in the journal I brought for her. And it is true

that she gave it back to me at the end of that first day, blank,
    that it took weeks for her to say, with reticence,
I hate white people, but you ain't like the white bitches
that run this place, and smile at me, for it is true that Dionna
rarely smiled, except when she was making small mischief,

like sneaking snacks in her lap under the common room table.
    And it is true that she refused to write in the journal—
she'd slide it across the table back to me week after week
after week, empty of the stories she dared not share,
full of the silences she felt compelled to keep.

But it is also true that three months in, she offered

to care for Shauna's sick daughter so Shauna could attend group
    because Shauna is a poet and Dionna says she's not.

And it is true that she made a mix CD for Ashley's birthday
and danced in the common room, bumping her butt up
against Ashley to make her laugh because her mother

could not come to celebrate with her. And it is true
    that she got in Q'nisha's face for pawning Angelica's
necklace before Q'nisha was sent away, Angelica sobbing
on the common room table. And it is true that when
the prompt was *Write a praise song for any of the mothers*

in the House, four of the women chose Dionna. And it is true
    that LaQuita said: *I like how Dionna don't take no shit*
from nobody, and that Brittany said: *Dionna alone in this world*
except for her babies, that Nicole said: *Dionna is strong*
and a good mother, that Shauna said: *She only like that because*

she hurt. You don't act mad at the world unless you hurt.
    And Dionna—who refused to write a praise song
because, she said, *I hate all of these bitches*—swatted at
her tears as the mothers read. She wiped her wet fingers
on her jeans under the table. We pretended not to notice.

The Room Toss Villanelle

The Haven House for Homeless Women and Children

You'd better wash your hands tonight.

You don't know what is hiding,
or even what you're looking for,

but this is your job, so you'd better do it right.

You've flipped through the children's
books the mothers read at night.

You've picked through baby clothes,
nudged open closet doors.

You'd better wash your hands tonight.

You've shoved your fingers in their shoes,
searched under mattresses with a flashlight.

You've rifled through their bedsheets,
scoured their underwear drawers.

But this is your job, so you'd better do it right.

You've peeked behind picture frames
for something to indict.

You've held necklaces to your chest,
wondered if they're paid for.

You'd better wash your hands tonight.

You've knocked things down
you've never placed upright.

You've left precious things overturned,
broken, or on the floor.

But this is your job, so you'd better do it right.

You've pored over the mothers' diaries,
their dreams' burial site,

and you've scoffed at the many things
they've said they're sorry for.

But this is your job,
and you know you've done it right.

Just make sure before you leave,
you scrub your hands clean tonight.

Ladies' Day at the Playhouse

For the mothers of the Haven House for Homeless Women and Children

Two River Theater, Red Bank, New Jersey, February 2013

MEMPHIS: You born free. It's up to you to maintain it. You born with dignity and everything else. . . . Freedom is heavy. You got to put your shoulder to freedom. Put your shoulder to it and hope your back hold up.

—August Wilson, *Two Trains Running*, act 1, scene 2

Hands grip painted rails as bodies and bodies climb
shallow stairs, file into aisles, thin out into row
after row after row like insects swarming a velvet maze.

The mothers pinch their tickets, show them to the usher as if
showing a license at the liquor store—proof of their
belonging there. The late sixties fixed as if behind museum glass.

A diner in Pittsburgh's Hill District stands still onstage:
a counter, stools, tables and chairs, a pay phone,
two booths, and a blackboard chalked with the menu.

We find our seats, eleven women split between two rows,
five in J, six in K, the bunch of us divided, but clumped together.
The mothers in back tug on our hair, tickle our ears, pull

the necklines of our sweaters. They snap selfies with their cell phones—
seats, set, and stage captured in the background—
and make megaphones and telescopes with their playbills.

The houselights so silver-bright the room feels almost holy.

Then, a man with a wristwatch and white hair stuffed in the conch
shells of his ears pushes down the seat next to me and eases
himself into the zigzag-patterned plushness, his knees falling open.

At intermission, this man will fling his playbill on the floor, hustle
his wife out, and huff: *I can't understand the way these people*
talk. I don't even know what they're saying. His exit will come

as no surprise because when he first sat down, he looked
at the women, then looked at me, then looked
at the women, then looked at me, and, seeing only dissimilarity,

with a smile he inquired, *Did you bring these girls here on a field trip?*
I hardened. *No, just a ladies' day at the playhouse*, I said.
I felt our two rows wilt, then the houselights blacked out.

Bastard Ghazal for the Death of SNAP

The Haven House for Homeless Women and Children

The 2009 Recovery Act's temporary boost to Supplemental Nutrition Assistance Program (SNAP) benefits is scheduled to end on November 1, 2013, resulting in a benefit cut for every SNAP household. For families of three, the cut will be $29 a month—a total of $319 for November 2013 through September 2014, the remaining months of fiscal year 2014. That's a serious loss, especially in light of the very low amount of basic SNAP benefits. Without the Recovery Act's boost, SNAP benefits will average less than $1.40 per person per meal in 2014.

—Center on Budget and Policy Priorities, August 3, 2013

The sound a whip makes on the hide of a steed—SNAP!—
to keep the needy in need, but enough to believe: SNAP.

They just changed the name, "Food Stamps" to "Assistance."
An Act renamed to stay the same. The "reconceived" SNAP.

Not Recover as in *restore*, but *cover again*.
Not Act as in *action*, but as in *make-believe*: SNAP.

To remove all the shame, the stigma of need
is to say no blood in bleeding when skin has been cleaved: SNAP.

Instead of stamps, plastic cards, what the public sees,
but separate bundles at the checkout, the public sees: SNAP.

Because EBTs don't cover diapers or cleaners,
or soap or toilet paper or Christmas Eve: SNAP.

In 2014, only $1.40 per mouth per meal.
A heavy burden for young mothers to heave: SNAP.

This is a poet's plea to Senator Reid.
Benefits will bleed. It's time to grieve the SNAP.

Welfare Mothers

The Haven House for Homeless Women and Children

LaQuita was chewing her cuticles when I noticed
how thin she had become, so careworn and thin. This afternoon,
her face was not its usual honey-gold, but gray—her hips thin,
wrists thin, all over thin. I asked her if she'd eaten today,
and with pink-rimmed eyes fixed on her fingers she shook her head.

I pulled eight singles from my jeans, bills as soft and worn
as used tissues, and held them out for her to take to the Wawa at the corner.
She held the money in a stiff gaze, but did not move until I took her wrist,
pressed the slim fold in her palm, and closed her fingers around it.
She returned with two bagels, a convenience store coffee,

a cherry Gatorade, a plastic knife, and one small cup of cream cheese.
I waited for the honey to return to her face as she ate and ate and ate.
With the last lump of food still stuffed inside her cheek,
LaQuita approached to give me a wrinkled Wawa receipt
and drop a dime, a nickel, and two pennies in my hand.

PART III
HOLY ORDERS

And whoever walks a furlong without sympathy walks to his own funeral, dressed in his shroud.

—Walt Whitman, *Song of Myself*, 48

Unto Others

To the roomful of people at the private fundraiser for Mitt Romney, May 2012

There are 47 percent who are with [the president], who are dependent upon government, who believe that they are victims, who believe that government has a responsibility to care for them, who believe that they are entitled to health care, to food, to housing, to you name it. . . . That's entitlement.

—Mitt Romney

All things therefore whatsoever ye would that men should do unto you, even so do ye also unto them.

—Matthew 7:12

Who is here so vile that will not love his country? If any, speak; for him have I offended.

—*Julius Caesar*, act 3, scene 2

Who there knows how good it is to know
a warm bed and a roof? If any, speak.

Who there knows how good it is to know
a schoolroom? If any, speak.

Who there knows how good it is to know
the stiffness of new shoes? If any, speak.

Who there knows how good it is to know
the steam of a meal on your cheeks? If any, speak.

Who there knows how good it is to know
some God hears you weep? If any, speak.

Who there knows how good it is to know?
All of you know, so speak.

Say you know how good it is to know.
All of you know, so speak. Say it's OK

for others to know how good it is to know.
Say it. Speak. You lose nothing

if others know how good it is to know.
Go ahead. Speak.

If you know how good it is to know,
why then don't you speak?

Why then don't you speak?
Say something. Speak. Speak. Speak.

PART IV
ANOINTING OF THE SICK

Touch me, touch the palm of your hand to my body as I pass,
Be not afraid of my body.

—Walt Whitman, "As Adam, Early in the Morning"

My Father Asks Me to Kill Him

When our neighbor rolled past,
or the mold of him, much older
from amyotrophic lateral sclerosis,
you noted, over your shoulder, how it's only

been a year. A year since he could hear
his name and nod, a year since he could
believe in a reason for being here,
on this beach street, alive, or seeming.

You looked at me. Something pushed up
through you like a wave of hooks. You took

your fingers, index and middle,
slid them underneath your chin, pressed
deeply, the skin sinking in,

cocked your thumb, locked and loaded,
blew your top off, rocked
your head back. Your lips popped

an imaginary gun. You made me say
I'd take your days away, your pain,
you made me say I'd shame you less

than a disease like ALS. Except, not a weapon.
Instead, a push down the steps or a deft wrench
of your neck, a heavy deck to your head.

I'd drop a drug in your blood, bludgeon
you till you're the ruddy muck of you,
stuff your head in the bathtub till the bubbles
won't come. Out of love, Father, out of love,

because you asked me to. I would
ruin you. Because you asked me to,
I would ruin you. Because you
asked me to, because you asked me to.

The Christmas Gift

I arrive at Pop's house a little early, holding a tray of cupcakes
with hard-sugar Santas and snowmen. *Merry Christmas!* I cheer.
My father hurries out from Pop's bedroom, shushing me,
waving one hand to stop me at the kitchen door. His other hand
    pinches with two fingers the handles of a plastic ShopRite bag,
looped and cinched like ribbons on a gift. He drops the bundle,

heavy and dark with his father's underpants, into the garbage can
and stomps the trash down. We wince at the climbing stench.
My father pulls up the Hefty bag from the can the way he used
to grip my clothes to lift and kiss me, then offers the bag to me.
He knocks the faucet up with his wrist to scrub his hands,
    says nothing, but jerks his head in the direction of the door.
Nodding, I tiptoe outside backwards, holding my tray and the trash,

and shiver on the stoop, waiting for enough time to pass, time
enough for a shower and fresh pants. And when I eventually reenter,
holding my holiday treats, my father cheers *Merry Christmas, baby!*
as if I had only just come in. He and I embrace—two players
    committed to this scene—as Pop shuffles from his bedroom,
ready for his kiss, clean and spry as a child on Christmas morning.

Never Too Late for Amazement

In memory of Paul Schmidt, 1918–2011

The day before Pop died,
he turned to his son
and whispered, with all
the breath his lungs
could summon,
How old am I?

When my father replied
Ninety-three,

Pop's eyebrows
arched their spines
as he shook his head
slowly, mouthed
the word *Wow.*

Grandpa's 70th Birthday

In memory of Michael Giovio, 1920–1997

For his 70th birthday, Uncle Smokey—
who was fined once for waving a dildo at a woman
in a car, who used to wake my mother by doing cannonballs
    on her in bed, who, for two miles, ran from his father
around the neighborhood for refusing to push in his chair
after being dismissed from the dinner table as a kid—

gives Grandpa a box of petrified cow shit and two nudie magazines.
The former because he lived on a Louisiana farm in those days,
the latter because, though Grandpa couldn't say much
    even nearing twenty years after his stroke, he loved
buxom women. Over cake, Smokey opens a magazine,
flashes pictures of naked women in his aging father's face:

Did ya ever learn to jerk it with your left hand, Mikey? he needles,
stroking a long cock of air at the dinner table. My mother smacks
her brother. *Fuckin' shit,* Grandpa huffs, shaking his head
    and waving his left, his one good hand.
Ya miss me? Smokey jests, knowing. *No, but yes,* Grandpa says.
After cake, my mother removes his bib and walks him

with his cane up the two steps to our side of the house.
We three kids are sequestered to our grandparents' kitchen
when the stripper arrives. Later, our parents let us watch
    the footage: first, she dresses Grandpa like Rambo—
she drapes a long, curly black wig over his head, a sash of plastic
bullets across his chest, and rests the butt of a machine gun

at his groin—then, she starts to take off her clothes.
Every time she removes a garment, the party hoots
and shakes noisemakers, but Grandpa just sits there,
    shaking his wigged head, half laughing, saying, *No-no, no-no.*
The stripper removes her shirt and Rambo says, *No-no, no-no.*
The stripper removes her shorts and Rambo says, *No-no, no-no.*

When she gets down to a mint-green bikini, Rambo holds up
clothes for her to put back on with his bumbling left hand.
No, but yes, he says. She shakes her head coyly at his offering.
    The family howls offscreen as she wiggles her breasts,
still in their bikini, near his face. Smokey's disembodied voice
sounds, *Ya like those, huh, Mikey?* Suddenly, the laughing stops:

Rambo starts to cry. Guarding her bikinied breasts,
the stripper hurries out of the shot as my mother rushes
to her father to wipe his tears away. The wig is crooked
    on his head now. He looks at her, helpless as a sick child,
Finished and finished? he says. She slides off the wig, fixes
his hair with her fingers: *Finished and finished*, she says.

The Nursing Home

Hackensack, New Jersey, May 1997

In the smell of wet shit and cafeteria food, husks of bodies
grow ever still on beds. Oil stains the shape of torsos,
    limbs, and heads soil sheets.

Splotches of black rot consume hamstrings
and buttocks. Pouches of piss, the color of copper,
    dangle from the backs

of wheelchairs, contraptions that look like claws
about to close around the soon-corpses
    cradled inside.

Room after room, the same snoozing bodies:
hands clenched shut by strokes or palsy, eyes half-
    closed in gobs of weepy glue,

tongues twitch and writhe like gray, salted slugs
as trays of food cool before toothless mouths.
    But in the common room,

seated at the upright Wurlitzer with a broken
lower G, I could feel hollow bodies
    walk themselves

in their wheelchairs into a crescent behind me,
a warm bass clef of sick breath and slow decay.
    All but one man gathered.

Instead, he rested his head on the table, left palm
down next to his ear. He never lifted his face, not for
    the woman who screamed

Elmo! repeatedly and raised her hands against
an imaginary attacker, not for the man
    who belted out songs

from *Hello, Dolly!*, not for the nurse who read
him passages from Genesis. Week after week,
    I would play long scales

of sonatinas, the minor chords of sonatas. Voices
would strain, near empty of breath, to hum along,
    yet he would never lift his head.

But today, at *Pachelbel's Canon*, his face still straight
down, I saw the man twiddle his fingers
    clumsily to the sound.

Silver Alert

For the random little old lady owner of the '82 green Toyota
Tercel, New Jersey license plate CDD013

This is an almost daily thing: the '82 Toyota
missing from the drive and Granny gone, too.

As rehearsed, the middle-aged daughter calls
the cops and the ladies from Mahjong Tuesdays,

then packs her kids in ski caps and jackets to circle
the neighborhood, all while Granny wheels along

the Parkway, blowing every toll. Maybe the tape deck
blasts The Platters as she sways between lanes

and blows kisses to the deer blinking at her
from a patch of grass near exit 102. Or maybe

she's on her way to the boardwalk to get a tattoo,
the first of her life, a hummingbird whose wings

flit so fast that all she ever saw was a shimmer
of green before it flashed away. Or maybe

this is the evening she made it all the way to Hackensack,
drifted to my grandfather's hospice room,

slipped into his in-three-days-he'll-be-dead bed,
her slippers on the wrong feet, and with a squishing

in her knickers, sang "Smoke Gets in Your Eyes,"
as she stroked the chin of a man she did not know

whose stroke-broken speech kicked and caught
like an old Toyota stolen for its last joyride.

Second Drink

For my grandfather, Michael Giovio, 1920–1997

On my pillow bit by bit waking,
suddenly I hear a cicada cry—
at that moment I know I've not died,
though past days are like a former existence.
I want to go to the window, listen closer,
but even with a cane I can't manage.
Before long like you I'll shed my shell
and drink again the clear brightness of the dew.
—Xin Oiji, "Start of Autumn: Hearing a Cicada While Sick in Bed"

On your pillow, bit by bit waking,
dreams of playground slides, highways, swatches of sky
all scatter into the fume of your first breath, waking.
Bit by bit, on your pillow, you wake

and suddenly you hear a cicada cry
from its flaky tomb. Caked in green, a fresh buzz breaking
the silence of an eight o'clock light, a clear cicada cry.
Suddenly, you hear a cicada cry,

and at that moment, you know you have not died.
Now, an armada of cicadas, in an apocalyptic quaking,
soars from the trees that have not died.
Neither, at that moment, have you,

though past days are like a former existence,
cast in a tomb, gilded in aching
like the words of a song that only in memory exists.
Future days, too, are like a former existence.

You want to go to the window, listen closer
    to the cicadas' rise, their resurrection, their remaking,
but your legs cannot bring you closer.
You want to go to the window, listen closer,

but even with a cane, you can't manage.
    Never in your daughter's dreams are your legs forsaken—
they're your wings, your wheels, your dream's imagining—
but even with a cane, you can't manage.

Before long, like the cicada, you'll shed your shell—
    your apocalyptic limbs regaining, reshaping—
stronger now than used to be. Strong like the cicada, you'll shed your shell.
Before long, like the cicada, you'll shed your shell

and drink again the clear brightness of the dew.
    You'll drink again the clear brightness of the dew,
and bit by bit, you will wake.

Exercises in Mourning

For my father on the days we spent cleaning out Pop's garage, December 2011

You said you know
that eventually
you'll have to
throw most
of the old photos
away—
no room
in your own home
to keep them—

but today,

we line the boxes
in a row,

push them
from the front
of Pop's garage
to the back,

back

to where
we pushed them from
just yesterday.

PART V
BAPTISM

Now I wash the gum from your eyes,
You must habit yourself to the dazzle of the light and of every moment of your life.

—Walt Whitman, *Song of Myself*, 46

The Box Marked "F"

For Michael

You grip your youngest son by his two ankles
    and peel him open from his diaper like a lid
        from a tin can. He is rolled back, his rubbery

bottom aimed at the sky so you can clean the ample
    spattering of shit between his cheeks. You get some
        on your hand, but this does not

bother you. By rote, you grab a fresh wipe,
    wring it between your palms like a mechanic
        ragging his hands after an oil change.

Your indifference to shit is no surprise to me,
    Brother, for you have always been crude
        and flatulent, unapologetic for either,

but, as you toss the fresh wipe away, you say
    it's going to be my responsibility to clean
        our parents' messes when they're old.

Though it will be years before our parents need wiping,
    you were much too quick to assign the filthy labor to me,
        the only daughter, the only box marked "F,"

the only one in the family who has no practice
    wiping anyone's ass but her own. Not even
        our other brother, aged between us—

who has two boxes marked “F” on top of his own to clean—
    is in line for the job. But before I can protest,
        I watch you palm a mixture of your son’s

snot and drool and smear it on the rug next to you.
    I imagine our parents, saggy and gray,
        scurrying to make it to the bathroom in time,

clutching their flat behinds, and I laugh because,
    brother—father to only sons—one day you will
        have to drag your ass along the carpet.

What I Learned about My Father One Day at the Beach in 1986

When the last bit of string slipped off the cardboard spool and my kite
sailed into the sky, lifting further and further away with each gust
of after-thunderstorm wind, I collapsed into the sand and screamed.

My father ran off the beach, then rushed north on the Boulevard,
the strip alongside the boardwalk which blinked with arcade lights,
sent smells of sausage sandwiches and zeppoles through the air.

My mother tried to appease me by sharing my brothers' kites while,
for two miles, my father hunted mine, all the way to Point Pleasant, stuck
to a moving bumper. When he returned, red and breathless, cheeks and chest

flecked with mud kicked up by the treads of the car he chased, he gave me
my mangled kite. We knew it would never fly again, but we took turns
running it till dinner anyway, laughing every time it came hurtling down.

Daughter

Ocean Beach, Toms River, New Jersey, Summer 2011

Clamshells wedge in wet sand so the whole beach
is a gleaming, cobbled walk. I hold a shell,
feel its heft and shine, finger the curve

of what's no longer living there. Just down beach, a seagull
snatches a little girl's sandwich from her hands
and soars away. She is on her toes now,

running in place and laughing. She squats down
next to her father, grabs his cheeks,
and aims his face at the bits of bread

falling from the beak of the thieving bird.
Her father forces the briefest interest, a crisp
shrug and wide-eyed nod, then returns

to the image on his phone. When she looks
at him, young as she is, she sees it. Too soon
such understanding comes—how it hinders

its own hope to be forgotten wholly, how it beds in her
chest like shell halves in sand so she is
a shiny thing, but heavy.

Memorial Park

When I returned to the baseball field of my girlhood,

I expected to see three fields and kids wearing uniforms:
    Bob's Deli, Krauser's, and Providence Bank,
the same sponsors that loved the game when I was twelve;

I expected to see the scoreboard with the lights
    blown out, the hot dog hut, and bleachers.

I expected Memorial Park to exist as if it were
    the year my Little League coach ordered the team
to hands and knees to scour the field for his wedding band.

(Our mitts dangled from our mouths as we examined
    each blade of grass for what we could learn
about growing up from the man who, nearly weeping,

hurled the bucket seats from his truck, tore at the floor mats,
    and tossed the contents of the glove box on the ground.
When a player's fist plunged up from the first base line,

Coach kissed his fingers and flung them at the sky.)
    But I never expected to find myself at twelve again:
flat on my back in the infield, a line-drive shot off my chest, bruised

and rolling, without breath. Clutching the sponsor on my heart,
    I waited for my father, who should have soothed me, who
should have touched me there, but couldn't, or didn't want to.

My Parents' New House, One Year after Hurricane Sandy

In the new house, my mother test-paints the walls
in the living room, dining room, and kitchen.
Paintbrush-width strips of six shades of beige
checker everywhere there is flat, white space.

In the living room, dining room, and kitchen,
my mother appraises the way sunlight plays on
the paintbrush-width strips of six shades of beige,
and she moves the new couch from place, to place, to place.

My mother appraises the way sunlight plays on
the many curtains, rugs, and pillows she's bought.
She moves the new couch from place, to place, to place.
She returns the curtains she's bought the very next day.

She buys more curtains, rugs, and pillows today.
If she likes these new ones better, she really couldn't say,
so she returns all she's bought the very next day,
but decides the couch is probably in the place it will stay.

If she likes one beige better, she really couldn't say.
It's been almost a year and still the checkers remain.
The couch is likely in the place it will stay.
But across the Toms River, her old home stands straight.

It's been more than a year and still the checkers remain.
She labors and labors to make this new place a home,
but across the Toms River, her real home stands straight.
If she likes the new house better, she really won't say.

In the new house, my mother test-paints the walls—
paintbrush-width strips of six shades of beige.
She will return the curtains she's bought the very next day.
But the couch is, at last, in the place it will stay.

Inheritance

Invariably,
when we left the house
on family trips

to the grocery store,
or vacations at the Jersey Shore,

my mother would turn to my father
in the front seat of the car, ask:

Did I leave the coffee pot on?

Invariably,
she didn't.

And because I don't
drink coffee,

I worry about my toaster.

PART VI
CONFIRMATION

Why should I wish to see God better than this day?
I see something of God each hour of the twenty-four, and each
moment then,
In the faces of men and women I see God, and in my own face in
the glass.

—Walt Whitman, *Song of Myself*, 48

Faith

After *Half Shorn Sheep*, photograph by Cary Wolinsky

But for Your sake we are killed all day long.
We are considered as sheep to be slaughtered.

—Psalm 44:22

A season's coat clothes the trunk
of a Merino sheep. One flank,

throat to breech, sheared clean.
The other, a full fleece three inches

deep. She stands—half-shorn, stiff,
and nicked—then sways before

capsizing, wool-side. She kicks her legs
to rise again, merely turns a deft circle.

Mother Teresa, Our Dearly Beloved Mother

These words they chipped into my stone chest,
but little else to say I soldiered for Christ. Badged,
I lived my life in the name of Christ, stormed
faithless troops on the frontlines for Christ.
Heavier is stone than wood. The Word,
    heavier still. And now,

when wind cuts across the letters' trenches
of my name, I hear the prayers that long since
    have fallen from my tongue.

For, in the evenings' darkest hours—
from when clock hands clasp upward in prayer
to the moments before morning's Christ
again rises—I looked up and saw
    not God, but nothing.

The Rapture

When they returned to shore after a day of fathers teaching sons
to fish, his father snapped a picture of him, his youngest son.

His adolescent back arched as if stabbed with a stroke of pain
to hoist, with a summons of strength, the black-painted

bass into view. Fingers slipped into the fibrous pink of the gill
half-unlock the body from the head. Meat hangs from hands like a sun-gilt

cloak from a hook. An old man now, this picture haunts his eyes.
Not the mouth unhinged as if caught mid-hymn, not the fish eyes

paused in their inauspicious gaze, or the blood dotting his hands and arms,
but a stranger in the background at the left. Six fish, armored

in stiffness, fall from his wrist, roped through gills and throats.
A bitch stands in a spill of black scales. The stranger throws

his eyes over his shoulder at the boiler of clouds about to close
around the sun. The beast noses at a fish. Others bleed beneath her claws.

Till Death

When I die, bury me in those earrings, the ones
you raked through an Exxon trash can,
filthy and bare-handed, to find—

two diamonds twisted in a tissue—
chucking half-chewed fast food
and gas slips over your shoulder.

When I die, cross my legs lotus-style, right over left.
I want to be stuffed in the ground this way
because it's how I'm most comfortable,

but if I'm going to be stuck in one position, love, I wish
it were under you. (Even though your body
weight caused chronic costochondritis

and your thigh draped over me once bruised
a rib in my sleep.) I know you'll want any
one day back, the way I wanted your

sidewalk chalk van Gogh after that August-warm
torrent took it from the drive.
I know you'll want to see me

in that dress again, the one I wore the night you didn't
have to ask because everything answered: *Yes.*
I saved the ease of the next day's waking for you

because when I die, dies with me the sleep you get
after hours at the beach, the sleep that drops you
off into the kind of darkness you need to feel

your way out of. I hate to say it, but you should give up
sweets because when I die, dies with me the day
a plum is perfect for eating. You can just forget

how good the grass feels, the air at seven in the evening
because it all goes, everything, with the heart
I gave you at fifteen. You carry it now,

I know, a pulsing, bloody mess in a tissue. But one day,
you'll pick through an Exxon trash can hoping
to return it to me—waiting

in the car, my face a rain-streaked *Starry Night*—
because, love, you're covered
in all I've left behind.

Before Grief

For my Googlegänger, Lauren Schmidt, Dubuque, Iowa, 1991–2007

There is no grief—
            it is too cold, too dark for that, too soon.

They are mulling it over in their heads,
      how tragic it is. Through tears, they are saying,
            There must be some mistake.

They are lowering themselves into dining room chairs
      with awful ease, covering their mouths
            as if to mute their shock will stop it.

They are asking all the *Why* questions that are proof
      no God exists, that the possibility of this earth,
            their lives, mine, were no more divine

intention than the moment the driver's eyes dropped
      from the road like the sun from the sky
            two hours too soon this time of year.

They are trying to muster the words for my brothers,
      who are already weeping into their sleeves.
            These are just the first responses.

There is no grief yet—
      that will come later. Soon,

they will finger the ripples in my sheets, the relief
      map of my dreams, smell the honey strands of hair
            still caught in the couch cushions. Soon,

they will clutch the clothes that hang
in my closet like skins of me,
like cottony, colored corpses. Soon,

they will take turns crying into the sweet-
heart neck of the prom dress I would
never get to wear. Soon,

they will shudder in the jamb to my room
and distribute to distant cousins its contents,
the seeds of my life's little growing.

Grief, though, real grief will come in spring
when the whole world reeks of my death
and hope wilts in its wake.

How wonderfully weak the human heart—
how I pity them for having one.
In death,

there is no grief—
it is too cold, too dark for that, too soon.

Of course, they do not know this.

Initiations

No one saw which boy made a nest
of the stranger's windshield.
    His reeling car sent a loud cry
crosswise into July silence.
Screen doors creaked, then clacked
    against their wooden frames.
Mothers cawed for their sons.

Sons scattered from bushes and ran
to their homes. The man rushed out
    of his car and clawed at the tufts
of hair just above his ears. Boys whizzed
past. My brother slinked through
    the kitchen door and scrambled
upstairs to his room. The break of

a lying boy's voice is as distinct as brick
blasting glass. As he fibs, his lip grows
    slick with a thin skin of sweat
and with rapid, heavy breaths, his chest
    lifts and sinks the way cracked glass
flexes without breaking all the way through.

When he was twelve, my brother tipped a cooler
on its side and a wave of sunnies he'd caught
    splashed onto the driveway. Shiny bodies
flipped and kicked as if on springs until
he crushed them with the tires of his Mongoose.
    Wet fish flesh caked his treads,
left a bloody trail on his afternoon ride.

When he was thirteen, I watched my brother
through the crack of his bedroom door,
    a sliver of him purpling his ribs with
his own two fists. With each hit, wings
flinched within his brows and tears swooped
    out from his eyes. *This is practice,*
I thought, but I did not know for what.

Parany

Casino Pier, Seaside Heights Boardwalk, 2011

Birdlime because the DO NOT TOUCH directive
taped to the neck of the headless mannequin
was not enough to keep the neighborhood of boy-
fingers from fondling her mannequin breasts.

Parany is illegal in most countries, but so is
public nudity, even if only long enough
for a wardrobe change, which is long enough
for a twelve-year-old boy to conjure the dare

for his friend, the friend who accepted, at age five,
the invitation to put a fistful of worms in his mouth.
But such is not a twelve-year-old dare because
by twelve, boys have discovered breasts, and by God,

why shouldn't they have discovered breasts? Breasts
on the covers of magazines! Breasts at the Super Bowl!
Tank tops wearing breasts! Beer cans frothing breasts!
Sports cars sporting breasts! All the world

abuzz with breasts, breasts, breasts! And what for?

So women can scorn these will-be-men-someday boys
who can't do much to ignore this glandular bait, so men
buy magazines with only pictures, get cruel looks
when it's cold outside and the breasts can't help but

announce it, so women have something to hold over men, literally
and figuratively both, so men—doing only what they know to do—
open their mouths to taste like birds awaiting their captors,
as they molt with frenzy, snagged on a sticky twig.

The Fourth of July

If I hadn't been sitting on my mother's lap,
I don't know that she could have smacked
out the orange embers that singed the sleeve

of my zip-up in time, before my jacket
went up in a wicked flame and our yearly
block-party-with-firecrackers-and-hot-dogs fun

at the Marcazies' turned tragic. And even though
she did smother the burns on my hoodie,
those were the days I was afraid of fireworks—

the pop they made when lit, the hiss as they soared
through the sky, the crack and bang, the way
even the softest summer wind would lift smoke

over our houses, our heads, the way ash trickled down
on our upturned faces, shiny with that great
and colorful light. I especially feared the ones

that released an almost animal scream as they scattered
in inestimable directions, the way we kids fled
from behind bushes playing Man Hunt in the after-

fireworks dark. Only a game of hide-and-seek,
but the stinging belts of terror in the chase
were as real as the scrapes on our knees

when we fell under the weight of the enemy
hands that crashed too heavily on our shoulders
in the tag. The next day, we'd find firecracker husks,

small round trunks, cluttering our lawns,
floating in our pools, flattened in the street
by Converse sneakers or cars. We found a cat

like that once, whipped by speeding wheels
and left behind. Not dead, but almost,
because, in those days—

when we played Contra and Commando
on our Ataris, when we tied yellow ribbons
around trees in our school yard, sang the revival

of "God Bless the U.S.A." for our parents' flashing
cameras, when we wore buttons on our chests
that said SUPPORT OUR TROOPS—

Mrs. Marcazie hoarded cats, and droves
of underfed beasts swarmed our streets,
scoured the dumpsters behind the apartments

for something forgotten to eat. Sometimes
they collapsed sideways from exhaustion.
Once, one of the big kids tried to plug the asshole

of a stray with a firecracker, but she screamed,
swiped straight for his eyes, and corkscrewed
out of his grip. Bounding away, she was

the amber flicker of light I sucked into a bowl
of weed the night the boys in my senior class
stuffed a firecracker into watermelon flesh

in the parking lot behind the Tom Sawyer Diner.
Peter dashed away from the pop of the lit fuse
and hopped into the Buick. Almost midnight

at the all-night eatery, we watched flesh splatter,
the spray of red wet fanning out from the round belly
of the fruit. Shards of the green-and-white-lined rind

dropped with the weight of a cat's paws. We cackled
as only kids can and careened away in our cars, waving
at the owner, who flipped us off from the emergency exit door.

Tonight, more than twenty years and four wars later,

in the middle of another war, I join my neighbors
on our beach street. We wait in anticipation for the show,
for that first pop and hiss, that scarlet crack

of light in the sky, and when the blasts begin,
together we gaze upwards, our eyes agog,
ice cream cones dripping down our knuckles.

On Route 208

a stretch of high-end cars
screeches to a stop
for a happy trail of ducks.
A near accident or two,
some flinging middle fingers
and angry late-day faces,
folks hurtling home
after eight hours
of coffee and telephones.

It pleased me to be
on that slice of highway
in the Garden State
that stopped
for the happy trail
because I think,
too often, we tend
to crush our ducks.

PART VII
HOLY ORDERS

I do not ask the wounded person how he feels. . . . I myself
become the wounded person.

—Walt Whitman, *Song of Myself*, 33

The Social Worker's Advice

The Haven House for Homeless Women and Children

Jabbing a finger at my face, you say, *You can't have*
empathy. Empathy will eat you alive, as if empathy
were a beast with feathers, fur, and hair, with hind legs
and deft feet, wings and claws, a beast that soars,
stalks, lunges, springs, a beast that chases, a beast
that screams instead of sings, with giant jaws
and a tongue budded with a rapacious taste for fools
like me, fools who don't believe the beast exists to eat,
who let it burrow its snout between our legs, fingers,
up to our armpits—the spaces of our common human stink.

But you see a beast that sniffs and snarls for a thick blue vein
to sic, and when I look at you I understand the beast more plainly—
I see that its skin collects pockmarks each time you dock
merit points to teach the mothers not to "talk Black,"
I see that its forehead sprouts a thousand of your scornful eyes,
its claws slash as swift and deep as your condescension—

because what you mean is that I can't have empathy
for these girls, for times like these, for a place like this,
for Nicole, who tallies the number of days it's been
since she last flushed her veins with a spoon-cooked mix,
twenty-eight days and counting. No empathy
for Nicole because she can never seem to find
matching socks for her four-year-old son, or because
she folds flowers from twice-used computer paper
to calm her nerves. Bouquets of paper daisies
sprout from vases on all four tables in the dining room.

What you mean is that I can't have empathy for Takina,
who was told to go by Tina because her white, adoptive
mother—middle-aged, middle-classed—prefers it.
Her birth mother is five years gone and Tina-Takina
thinks she might be pregnant again. I can't have empathy

for Denice who is pregnant with her third, but didn't know
until she was too far in, for Angelica who fell down the stairs
while holding her infant son, too spent from pre-sun
feedings and weeping in the wee hours as minutes lurch by.
Each ticktock is the sound of the deadlocked door
of the nighttime aide who snores in the small room
near the exit like a beast at the gates, preventing escape
from this place, this time, from lives like these
without signing a release form for the Division of Youth
and Family Services, like Dionna, who took her two kids
to a hotel, where, alone, at night, she stares at ceiling holes
in the red glow of the word VACANCY flashing through
windows with no curtains. I can't have empathy for LaQuita,
so thin that when she aims her breast at her baby's lips,
she prays she has something wet and real to give.

When you say, with your wagging finger, *You can't have
empathy. Empathy will eat you alive*, what you mean
is that I can't have empathy for these girls, and when I look
at you, I cannot help but wonder when you first believed
empathy would do more than sniff and lick your palms.

So, I say, let it take me, then, this beast of your invention,
let it slip its fangs into my skin and tear through my throat,
let it suck all the fat and blood from off my solid bones.

PART VIII
COMMUNION

To touch my person to some one else's is about as much as I can stand.

—Walt Whitman, *Song of Myself*, 27

Trial by Onions

To measure my teenage father's devotion to my mother,
Grandpa invented tests. Once, while driving through a field
    behind a farmer's truck, he glanced in the rearview mirror,
said, *Hey, Donnie, why don't you pick up some of those onions?*

Dutifully, my father hung out the door of the moving Chevy,
his white-blonde hair shimmering in the sunlight, to collect the onions
    that rolled off the back of the truck for his future father-
in-law. One by one, the boy tossed yellow bulbs in the back seat

while Grandpa's eyes gleamed in the sideview, half watching,
half driving. And if not catching onions, it was mowing the lawn,
    trimming hedges, cleaning the garage, or picking weeds
in the garden. When I asked my father why he would put up with this—

since he was only sixteen and Grandpa was well in those days
and had a teenage son to boot—he held his palms
    in front of his chest as if weighing two honeydews,
and grinned, *Your mother had the most amazing tits!*

Receiving

My mother used to share wads of peanut butter
off a spoon with our dog, and I couldn't get over
    how to drink blood from a chalice with a church-
ful of strangers. The little napkin ministers used
to pinch the drink's rim clean was not a suitable

measure of preventative health, so I'd fall in line
behind my mother, whose mouth was indiscriminately
    faithful, who once ate the host off the floor after it fell
from an old woman's lips, tongue-slicked side down,
no doubt, wet with a stranger's spit, the mist

of a stranger's prayer. When I asked my mother why
she didn't pick up the host and give it to the woman, why
    she pressed it to her tongue and crossed herself instead,
she said, *It would have been a sin not to receive it*
the way it had been given to me. I always cupped my hands,

held them out for the offering—my faith neatly packaged,
delivered in a way I could understand, though its message
    wholly lost on me, especially on Sunday evenings,
when our priest came to our house to give my stroke-broken
grandfather Communion. I'd watch him labor to follow

the priest's prayers—a series of babbles and the occasionally
well-landed *Amen*—before Father O'Brien would place
    the round wafer on Grandpa's tongue, lift blood
to Grandpa's lips. Only old people opened their mouths
for the Eucharist. I remember being told that the way

to receive Christ's body was not to chew it, but to push
the unleavened flesh with my tongue to the roof of my mouth
until it dissolved there, but in our kitchen—
Christ's house everywhere—Grandpa would chomp the body,
which seemed appropriate for a man with this body: dead

right arm, dead right leg, limbs like crosses he dragged through
more than two decades before dying, not many words other than
shit, *fuck*, *goddammit*, and *douche bag*. My father told me that,
as the soon-to-be new man of Grandpa's house, he sent away one
of Grandpa's sisters from the kitchen days after his stroke for laughing

at him crying, trying to make words, and fumbling a fork
with his left hand. We three kids came not long after,
and in family pictures, Grandpa holds us tightly on his left leg,
snug in the crook of his left arm like little pink footballs.
There are Christmas pictures, pictures of him leaning over,

laughing because he's about to fart, pictures of us kissing him
on the lips, the way the next generation of kids kiss us
on the lips now, but there is an age when this will change,
when the children will twist spastically away, swat at our lips,
or run for cover. *The only kiss on the lips my father ever gave me*

as a woman, my mother once said, *was on my wedding day.*
There is a picture of this in our house, a slightly side-of-the-lips
kiss because my mother, a bride of just twenty,
didn't know how to receive it, the last kiss from her father
while he was still well on her last day in her father's house.

Two years later, she would return to her father's house,
her three children born and raised in her father's house. And though
she does not say this, my mother wishes she had not
half refused her father's kiss—she keeps that pang pressed
to the roof of her mouth, waiting for it to dissolve.

Communion

Tonight you are gone, though your cockfunk-and-come scent
lingers in my sheets, your dishes still sit in my kitchen sink,
your T-shirts wrinkle in my hamper. I am alone in this bed
listening to my neighbor tinker on his guitar. Without you,

I am comforted by the slim distance between these rooms—
his, mine—a space wide enough to afford us our air
of detachment, but not so wide to spare us the intimacies
we're careful not to confess when we cross paths on the porch:

how the stiff spring of his morning piss sometimes wakes me,
the stink of skunked beer, how our utility bills rest their heads
together like lovers before departing, how I can hum along
to the only song he knows on the guitar, the thrumming
body he huddles over when the night grows cold enough.

Cloistered

The Haven House for Homeless Women and Children

There are no men in the Haven House.
And whether it was the tides and the moon

or the nearness of their rooms, ten red rosaries
aligned, and the animal throb of their bodies

too hard for two mothers to deny, so when
I say, *Write a poem about a body you know*—

bodies of their sons, their daughters,
their mothers, their own—Shauna writes

of the night she made her way into a bedroom
down the hall, and reads aloud her poem

about the dark vinegar of another woman's
menstruation on her mouth, the tang of that

first forbidden taste. She reads about how
the scent of red-brown silt streaked her nose,

chin, and cheeks, how her fingernails carried
crescents of blood for three days before the smell

they held was fully scrubbed away, how she'd lift
her fingers to her nose to inhale, teasing her secret

lover in the hallways and over dinner. But here
she is now, the door to her confessional wide open.

All other mothers but one are scared. Of what,
it is not clear: the blood, the body, two bloods,

two bodies, sex at all in a place where you can't
even snack in the living room, sex because

sex put them here in the first place, though
not this sex, hidden sex, between-two-

women sex, at-that-time-of-the-month sex,
with-the-nighttime-aide-just-downstairs sex,

there-are-no-men-in-the-Haven-House sex,
so two women turned to each other, bowed

to the cross of the other woman's body,
and drank deeply of her consecrated wine.

Some Joy

The Haven House for Homeless Women and Children

come celebrate
with me that every day
something has tried to kill me
and has failed.

—Lucille Clifton, "won't you celebrate with me"

When Anna comes to count the mothers' heads,
check off names, scribble across DYFS forms,

she tells Brittany to leave, the son in her arms
contraband in the common room. She looks at me

with weary, angry eyes, says, *I ain't leaving. Tell her*
I can stay, but before I do, Anna huffs out

of the room, clipboard hard against her chest.
Double-fisted middle fingers and silent, long-held

Fuck yous are aimed at the door. Shauna gets up
and locks it, hisses, *Stupid bitch*. They cackle

at this minor coup. As we read the day's poems,
Brittany pulls a sack of McDonald's from her bag—

more forbidden goods—chews bits of briny meat and holds
the mush out for her son to take with his gooey,

toothless mouth. I watch her eyes light at this
communion, the pens swaying in furious

movement like flags after the revolution, and I can see
    that too many days here have mixed cruelty

with beauty, have forced from these girls gratitude
    for the slenderest blessings, like this one,

when they remind each other of their spines,
    their eyes. When they demand it—some joy—

it is given to them in perhaps no greater miracle
    than that they can find it here at all.

Expectations

The Haven House for Homeless Women and Children

For you, Brittany

In your journal you write, *My mama say she gave me a white girl name,*
so I could one day get a good job and have a better life than hers.

My mother wanted to name me Donnaire or Arleen—
Donnaire because she heard the name once and loved it,
Arleen because her then best friend was Arleen.
For a time before I was born, I was a Laura
like my great-grandmother, who laughed through her nose
and ate lemons, she said, so she could live until
she was a hundred. Laura died at ninety-four.
But when I came into the world, my mother's
obstetrician proposed *Lauren*, and my parents signed the name
to my certificate. They signed their names on either side.

My mother said she knew exactly when she conceived me,
as if I were a dream she made up with her own body, as if
she willed me here, her little girl. I imagine the two of them—
my father, twenty-six with two sons, two jobs, tired from
tending bar, lying with his wife in bed, stroking the half basketball
beneath her cotton nightie, and my mother hugging the underside
of her belly, beaming at her high school sweetheart husband.
I imagine the two of them breathing me into being, each saying,
I hope she has your eyes or *Definitely, your sense of humor*,
assigning to me the best they see in themselves.

Instead, your mother named you Brittany, trying not to see
the food stamps, the too-thin walls, and the empty side

of her bed. In Brittany, she saw an aunt and a grandmother,
on the night of your birth, get trapped in a department store
buying you dresses—too busy holding up tiny plastic hangers
with pink frills and white flowers, too busy cooing to note
that the store had already closed. In Brittany, she saw a baby girl
who took nearly two years to walk because nobody in the family
could bear to put her down. She saw birthday cakes, graduations,
a big white wedding where your father would give you away.

Today, a mother now, you write that people will never see you
as a Brittany. They say
you're more Latasha or Danisha,
more Aiyesha or Kianna,
more Shirelle or Shonda. They say
you're more Latoya than Lily,
more Deondra than Brianna,
more Kadijah than Courtney.

But you, Brittany, you say,
If they don't expect me
to be what I am,
I'll blow they minds
in more ways than one.

Brittany's Tattoo

The Haven House for Homeless Women and Children

Her tattoo is no stone-cold Lady Justice—
tattered blindfold, sword, scales in balance—

just the ink-black cursive word
Justice cutting over the upward

thrust of her jugular—
from her throat to the jug band

of her heart to the ovation
of her brain stretches that thin, blue tether.

Only *Justice*
because when Brittany needs to believe
the word's wine-red truth, she presses

that wormy vein to feel blood
thunder beneath her fingers.

PART IX
HOLY ORDERS

Failing to fetch me at first keep encouraged,
Missing me one place search another,
I stop some where waiting for you

—Walt Whitman, *Song of Myself*, 52

Looking for Whitman

For Martín Espada

Camden was originally an accident—but I shall never be sorry I was left over in Camden! It has brought me blessed returns.

—Walt Whitman

What would Whitman think of what used to be Mickle Street,
where stoops and sidewalks erupt with the roots
of teetering trees, where parking meters, leaning
in a slate-gray sky, wait, their mouths open for dirty change,
where buildings, seared with spray paint, slouch
in the city heat, where storefront windows are patched
with planks of wood, where letters of street signs have slipped
off, where stoplights don't blink, where streetlamps are busted out?
What would he think of the cardboard clock pressing its face
against the window to his home, a timepiece with plastic hands?
Next tour: one o'clock, the red hands say.

What would Whitman think of his death notice, now framed,
that hung on the front door, never having seen it himself?
What would he think of you and me, the future readers
he wrote for, or the tour guide who wanted only to return
to his turkey sandwich? Did Whitman know you
would point to the title page of the first edition
of *Leaves,* where the poet's name, strangely, is missing?
What would he think of John Giannotti's gargantuan statue,
the falsely reverent pose, the vest, the cane, the butterfly
perched on the bronzed finger? Would the poet really approve
of standing outside the Rutgers campus Starbucks?

What would Whitman think of the prison across the street
from where he died on the other side of the boulevard
named today for Martin Luther King? What would he think
of the chained fences, how they wear wreaths of barbed wire?
What would he think of the dusty field in the back, where men
once scuffed their feet while walking aimlessly in the dirt,
or scratched their names with the toes of their shoes?

What would Whitman think of Haddon Avenue,
the long stretch south to where he rests, the buildings,
pocked with gunshots, gang tags searing every
flat surface, or the flags that hang like a death notice
for the city's doors, from the top of every streetlight?
Tomorrow is a new day, the red flags say.

What would Whitman think of Camden, a city
that has forgotten him, a city where the only haven
from death along Haddon Avenue is Harleigh Cemetery?
What would he think of the rain that fell
on my umbrella, rapping like gunfire?
What would he think of you jokingly quoting his line
about boot-soles when I slipped on slick roots,
snakelike and wild as the poet's own beard?

What would Whitman think of the padlock that sags
from the thick chain wound around the spires of the iron gates—
the door he wanted open so his soul could roam free?
What would he think of the trees that bow their heads
to kiss his triangular tomb, or the poets and dreamers
who come to carve their names in the guts of the trunks
the way a prisoner scars the walls of his cell?
I was here, those names say. *Let me be remembered.*